Memories of Rochda[le]

Foreword

Memories of Rochdale is not intended to be a history book - it has much more to do with entertainment than serious study. Most, if not all of the photographs featured here have one thing in common; they have been chosen to rekindle memories of times not-so-long ago in the minds of people living in or around the Rochdale area.

The compilation of *Memories of Rochdale* has been a very enjoyable experience for me. The book is the latest in a series of about a dozen similar publications covering towns and cities in the Lancashire and Yorkshire area. What has made this book special is the support and assistance I have been given by many local people. All proud and enthusiastic about the history of their town, and all private individuals with other demands on their time, but every one of them willing to find the time to help prepare this book, so that their fellow townsfolk could enjoy some pictures from the past which would otherwise remain unseen. Unusually for me, this book has relied entirely upon the assistance of this small army of helpers for its editorial content - not public institutions which are a more typical source of help. Overall, I think that the book is fresher and more varied because of this, and the friendship I have struck up with so many helpful and interesting people has made me a lifelong fan of Rochdale. *Memories of Rochdale* has been written for people who live in the present but enjoy looking back on the past.

I hope that you enjoy reading the book as much as I enjoyed compiling it.

Phil Holland
Publisher

The nearest that Rochdale got to a Flying Squad? PCs Bell and Bollington with their high speed pursuit vehicle (!) in 1955.

Published in December 1996 by:
True North Publishing,
Dean Clough Industrial Park,
Halifax, HX3 5AX.   Telephone 01422 344344
Repro. by Transgraphic Ltd., Morley.
Printed by Joseph Ward ColourPrint Ltd., Dewsbury.

true north PUBLISHING

ISBN No. 1 900463 60 1

£4.99 (nett)

Memories of Rochdale

Contents

Acknowledgments

I am delighted to acknowledge here the invaluable help I have received from some marvellous people in Rochdale, Whitworth and Littleborough in compiling this modest book. In alphabetical order, they are: Clifford C. Ashton, the well known press photographer who has a superb collection of work spanning around sixty years. Clifford supplied the majority of the photographs featured here and the quality of his work really brings the pages alive. Colin Atkin - a real expert and enthusiast on many local sports - and helped us with the history of the *Hornets* in particular. Eric Bollington, whose photograph can be seen on the previous page, showing Eric and a colleague in police uniform, was good enough to allow me access to his extensive collection of postcards, as well as pointing me in the direction of other people mentioned here who helped me in many ways. A special thank you too, to Alex France, Jack Foster and their colleagues at the Whitworth Historical Society Museum at North Street, Whitworth, for the use of several excellent pictures and endless, patient assistance. Richard S. Greenwood - an expert in many fields (though he won't thank me for saying that) found time to supply photographs and information, despite the many demands on his time, and he deserves my thanks. Allan Marshall stepped in at the last minute and lent me some of his photographs from the 1960s, along with supporting information including a copy of *his* book, *In The Beginning And Later,* which I would recommend to anyone interested in the origins and development of this area.

Mention must be made too, of the support we have had from the advertisers contained within the book. Most of them have been established in Rochdale for a large number of years and feel as passionate about the town as any of us. Their involvement has made it possible for us to sell the book at a modest price and we are grateful to them for that. Finally, Gareth Martin and Mandy Walker worked hard to organise and typeset the advertisements in *Memories of Rochdale* and I am very happy to acknowledge their assistance here.

Memories of Rochdale is dedicated to Livia Nicholson, a truly lovely person with strong Rochdale connections.

Wheels in motion

Right: July 1962, and a party of youthful train-spotters 'cop' yet another 'Dub-Dee' freight engine on an empty coal train bound for Yorkshire, while a stopping passenger train from Liverpool gets ready for departure headed by a 'Crab'.

Below: A diesel train for Leeds came to grief in Castleton station and a steam engine had to be called in to remove it. The strangely shaped buildings in the background behind the diesel train were Maltings Warehouses belonging to Magee Marshall brewers of Bolton.

Below, right: A familiar view to many thousands of local travellers - the interior of Rochdale station - advertising the fare to Blackpool at just 5s 6d

Memories of Rochdale

Left: Castleton station in May 1964.

Below, left: In the days before trams took to the streets one of the few forms of public transport was the horse-drawn bus such as the one pictured here. In this scene, a group of 15-20 young men are about to embark on a trip to Chester for a picnic in 1911. Goodness only knows how long it would have taken them to get there - and back!

Below: A marvellous photograph of a single-deck tramcar. Trams had first appeared in Rochdale in 1882 in steam-powered form, and these were eventually replaced by cleaner, more efficient electrically operated vehicles in 1905. Motorbuses eventually proved the most popular method of transporting the public, and these took on the task from the 1930s.

Memories of Rochdale

Right: A number of railway enthusiasts from the Rochdale area collected funds to preserve a Lancashire and Yorkshire Railway 'Pug' engine - one of the smallest locomotives to work on B.R. In 1967 the engine was exhibited as part of the Rochdale Model Railway Exhibition held at the Fire Station Hall. The picture shows the engine as it was being taken to the Worth Valley Railway at Haworth, to Newton Heath Shed, to work an enthusiasts special from Rochdale to Whitworth.

Below: Nostalgia guaranteed for anyone with memories of Rochdale railway station.

Photos supplied on this and opposite page by Richard S. Greenwood

Memories of Rochdale

Left: Market Street, Whitworth, and a busy scene outside the Dog and Partridge Public House (the building on the right of the picture) involving and open-topped electric tram and around thirty local children with a handful of adults looking on. At this time (around the turn of the century) the chance to have one's photograph taken would have been seized upon by all all concerned. Note the footwear on the children - nearly all of them in clogs or heavy boots - and most of them wearing a hat of some sort too.

Right: Ready...steady.......have your picture taken.......GO! These eager cyclists were preparing to race at Whitworth Cricket and Football Ground when the photograph was taken in September 1897. They were members of the well-known Rossendale Bicycle and Tricycle Club. Fortunately, for us couch potatoes, someonc invented television sometime between then and now, so that middle-aged men no longer have to resort to this kind of thing to while away a few hours.

Memories of Rochdale

Right: A proud moment captured on camera. The Whitworth coach firm owned and operated by Charles Holt and Sons was well known to everyone in Whitworth, Rochdale and beyond. Excursions by coach were popular in the days before most families had access to a motor car, and Bank Holidays and local works holiday periods would draw coach operators into Rochdale, Whitworth and Littleborough from miles around - all offering trips to the coast or other beauty spots to the thousands of very willing passengers in the area.

Left: A sponsored cycle ride by regulars at the Cock and Magpie public house in Whitworth. The ladies concerned look as if they're having much more fun than the gentlemen on the bikes on the opposite page. The scene was captured in April 1981, and the lovely ladies were sure to have brought the quiet streets of Whitworth to a standstill with their snazzy outfits. Where are they now, we wonder?

Memories of Rochdale

Above: A wintry flurry during the afternoon of December 5th 1961 as two Rochdale Corporation buses line up on South Parade with the Regal Cinema just across the way.

Above, right: This photograph was taken in 1905 and shows the last of the steam trams (right of the picture) and one of the first of the electrically powered vehicles.

Right: Some of the first motor cars to grace the roads of Rochdale are seen here outside James Clegg's Station Garage situated on Tweedale Street.

Memories of Rochdale

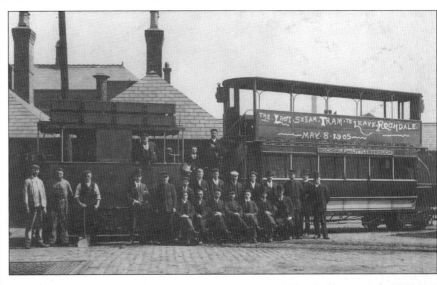

Right: This snow scene was captured on Whitworth Road - opposite Thrum Hall Lane, just above the Albion Hotel in the late 1950s. Clifford C. Ashton was the photographer in question - he took this photograph for one of his many national newspaper clients who was keen to show how us brave northern types cope with a bit of snow.

Above, right: A commemorative postcard entitled 'the last steam tram to leave Rochdale in May 1905'. It is a sobering thought to think how many of the upright workers pictured here would have been worried sick about losing their job as a consequence of the arrival of the all new electric trams. The more things change, the more things stay the same...

Above: A familiar sight. Broadway just after the trams had gone, thought the tracks and overhead lines remain.

Shopping Spree....

Left: Yorkshire Street, characteristically crowded with shoppers in this photograph from the late 1960s, and showing the still uncompleted rebuilding of the Market complex after the 1937 fire.

Below: G. Wild was a successful jeweller and pawnbroker in Rochdale and his premises dominate this photograph of Lord Street looking towards College Street with the Seven Stars Hotel in the distance.

Memories of Rochdale

Left: Toad Lane after the partial rebuilding of the market site after the disastrous fire of 1937 in this photograph from 1965.

Below: The magnificent and imposing building housing the main Pioneers Co-op Store at the junction of St. Mary's Gate and Toad Lane.

March 1967, and a busy shopping scene on South Parade, The Butts and The Walk.

Memories of Rochdale

Market life 100 years ago

The clarity of this photograph belies the fact that it was taken over 100 years ago, in 1895. It shows the Old Clock Face in the background and the open market on the right. The photograph is unusually atmospheric as a consequence of the subjects in the scene being totally unaware that the photographer was at work. Again, unusually, there is very little blurring of the figures in the picture who are busy getting on with their daily lives. All in all, a beautiful old photograph.

Memories of Rochdale

Right: This picture is over 60 years old and may be familiar to a small number of people in the Rochdale area who used to frequent the covered market before it was lost in the well known fire.

Below: The Open Vegetable Market at the junction of Lord Street and Toad Lane, pictured here in the 1930s prior to the 1937 fire which devastated the Closed Market which can be seen in the background.

999 - Emergency!

Left: A spectacular scene captured by Clifford C. Ashton in March 1969 when a serious fire swept through the College of Art - formerly the Rochdale Central School. The photograph magnificently recreates the atmosphere of the night - you can almost smell the smoke and hear the cracking of the timbers as the flames ripped through the building - entirely characteristic of Ashton's top quality photography.

Below: The aftermath of the fire at the Theatre Royal in November 1954 and we see a lone Fireman damping down the twisted remains of the once-beautiful building in which so many thousands of townsfolk had enjoyed many happy hours over the years.

DANGER - LOW BRIDGE

Below: Oops. This unhappy outcome was the result of a Rochdale double-decker bus attempting to pass under a low bridge near the railway station on Milkstone Road in 1974.

Right: The twisted steel girders and useless spinning machinery perched precariously above the devastation caused in this major fire at Clover Mill, make for an erie scene in 1952. Incredibly, close inspection of the spinning equipment reveals them to be still threaded up for work - despite the intensity of the heat which had been fierce enough to bend the girders below like sticks of toffee.

One dead and fourteen injured in Athletic Grandstand tragedy...

Despite the tragic death of one fan and injuries to fourteen others, most people were amazed that the casualty toll was not much higher when the grandstand collapsed at the Athletic ground in 1939. Salford were playing Wigan in the Cup semi-final at the time and the roof of the stand was weighed down with fans eager to secure a suitable vantage point for the important match.

These photographs were taken by Clifford C. Ashton and used by many national newspapers throughout the country on the day after the tragedy. The pictures were taken by a camera using large glass plates, and Clifford recounted how he had only taken about half the number that he would normally take to a match because he was booked for a wedding that weekend. He managed to use the plates he had effectively though, as we can see here.

Above: The Butts House, used as offices by Kelsall and Kemps and later the site of the Regal Cinema, and after that the Ritz Bingo Hall. This was a popular landmark in the centre of town for many years.

Left: Packer Street, Rochdale in a photograph dating back a staggering 130 years to 1866. Overlooking this slum area is the Parish Church - complete with the clock face which was removed in 1873. The Church dates back to Norman times.

Memories of Rochdale

Left: Provisions were taken by sledge to Red Lumb village in 1953.
Below, left: Sheep being led to safety near Edenfield Road.
Below: Digging out the snow-plough on Edenfield Road near Red Lumb, again in the winter of 1953.

The driving force behind Internal Mixers for over 100 years

Founded over 100 years ago, Carter's main product was originally Transmissions and Line Shafting for textile machinery in the then thriving cotton industry of Lancashire. With the gradual decline of this industry it became apparent that diversification was essential for the company to survive. A decision was made to enter the field of rubber and plastic processing machinery.

The introduction of the Internal Mixer and its rapid deployment, saw Carter's on the road to becoming specialist engineers to the rubber and plastics industry. For fifty years, Carter Bros were involved in the building and repairing of Internal Mixers, and before long it was only natural that Carter Bros developed their own brand of Internal Mixer.

Carter Brothers (Rochdale) Ltd is located just a mile from Rochdale town centre and just a few minutes away from the beautiful North England countryside and moorland.

Their offices and factories cover approximately 150,000 sq. ft., situated only three miles from the motorway network and 30 miles from Manchester (Ringway) Airport. This makes it extremely convenient for overseas and national clients.

Just as the name Carter Bros. is synonymous with Lancashire, so is the name Jon Fletcher. Jonathon Bridge Fletcher is the chairman and managing director of Carter Bros. He began his career with Carter Bros in the late 60s. He has been the driving force behind Carter Bros., which has seen the company emerge from the recession to become a leading force in the world today.

In the 1960s, some of the Bridge family, who were in business for themselves, opted to leave their company and purchased Carter Bros. Ultimately, this led to Jon Fletcher joining the company and by sheer hard work and ability, progressing to chairman and managing director in the 80s. Besides all this, Jon is well known in the racing circuits around Britain and quite a few trophies take pride of place in his living room.

Today, Carter's machines are regarded world wide as the most advanced and efficient machines on the market. A skilled and experienced workforce have drawn on a wealth of knowledge acquired over the years to produce the Mixers with optimum designs for efficiency and durability.

Above: Jon Fletcher, chairman and managing director of Carter Bros.

Left: One of Carter Bros' renowned Internal Mixers.

Royal visits

Rochdale was chosen for a Royal visit in 1954. Her Majesty the Queen and his Royal Highness the Duke of Edinburgh stopped off as part of their tour of Lancashire towns during that year.

These charming photographs capture the Royal couple looking natural and relaxed, and are the work of local photographer Clifford C. Ashton. The picture on the left shows the the Royal couple talking to Lord and Lady Derby as they look up the platform of Rochdale station for the man with the green flag.

Memories of Rochdale

Below: The crowds turned out for this visit of the Duke of Kent in 1936. The Duke called in at two social service centres on Milton Street and Smith Street which had achieved national fame for their achievements.

Above: The balcony of Rochdale Town Hall gave the citizens of the town a rare but valuable glimpse of Her Majesty Queen Elizabeth when she visited Rochdale as part of a tour of Lancashire and the north of England. In the days before television news coverage and *Hello* magazine, Royal visits had a special significance to the public - after all, apart from the newsreels, it was the only time they could get a clear view of the popular family.

Birds eye view....

Left: This aerial photograph records the way that the centre of Rochdale looked almost thirty years before the time of writing, the year being 1969. Most of the familiar landmarks can be made out - the Town Hall on the middle-right with Broadway in front of it, the College buildings and the cricket ground at the bottom left of the picture, and the modern high-rise flats above them. It gives an interesting view of the river snaking across the picture and up to where it is covered over under Broadway, and the contrast between the older buildings and their newer neighbours here is quite marked.

Right: A tremendous find - this print from 1938 showing town centre Rochdale just before the Second World War and before many of the changes that we are familiar with today. High quality copies of these aerial photographs are available from the publishers of this book.

Memories of Rochdale

Our Gracie ...

No book about Rochdale would be complete without a tribute to her most famous daughter Gracie Fields. She is seen here singing to her fans from the Town Hall balcony in October 1954. Clifford C. Ashton captured the scene using a flash from a hand-held powder flash of the kind most of us have seen in old movies. He tells the tale of how he used 20 times the normal amount of powder for the photo - dazzling the people here and lighting up half of Rochdale in the small explosion that followed!

Memories of Rochdale

Right: Gracie Fields was born *Gracie Stansfield* at this modest house on Molesworth Street. The building was demolished many years ago. Gracie Fields was loved by millions of fans throughout the world and her proudest moment was when she received the Freedom of the Borough of Rochdale in May 1937.

Below: This unusual photograph is typical of the fun-loving side of Gracie Fields' nature and her willingness to accommodate the wishes of her fans and photographers to create a picture with a difference. It was taken in Rochdale by Clifford C. Ashton in 1937.

Civic symbols

Much has been written about about Rochdale's best known building, the imposing Town Hall and her magnificent clock tower.

The building was opened in 1871 and cost £155,000 to construct - a massive sum at the time. Over the years the area surrounding the Town Hall was improved gradually to give the location the space necessary to show the building off to its best advantage. The original clock tower was made from timber and, perhaps predictably, was the unhappy victim of a major fire which destroyed all 240 feet of it in 1883. Four years later the present stone tower (which enjoys a much less elaborate design and is some 50 feet shorter than the original structure) was built a few yards to the east of the original spot. This photograph was taken in September 1956

Memories of Rochdale

Right: This photograph was taken in the late 1860s and shows workmen hoisting the huge timber roof supports into place in the Town Hall. It is difficult to imagine the scale of the task involved in this kind of construction work which was done without the assistance of powerful overhead cranes and winches. Minutes after this photograph was taken the ropes snapped and sent the heavy beams crashing through to the Mayor's parlour below.

Below: The White Angel was presented to *Rochdale* by Ellen Mackinnon in 1899 in memory of her mother. They did that kind of thing in those days. The monument served as a drinking trough for horses and dogs, but had a far more exciting reputation as *the place* in Rochdale for courting couples to meet.

Mayor's Procession, 1910.

This rare photograph shows the Mayoral Procession as it approached the camera on its way along Broadway in 1910.

Keen-eyed readers may just be able to make out the top-hatted Mace Bearer walking just in front of the Mayor and the escort of around ten local constables just ahead of the main party. The single-deck electric tramcar just off centre has the destination 'Bury' displayed upon the front of it and the building on the right of it is a tram shelter. The facility survived until 1933 when it was demolished. The Mayor's Procession was obviously an event to be taken seriously by the people of Rochdale, judging by how smart everyone in the picture is dressed.

Memories of Rochdale

If ever a picture could evoke memories of the 1930s in Rochdale, then surely this is it! This view shows Broadway with the Town Hall, the recently built Post Office building on the corner of Newgate and the Cenotaph (designed by Sir Edward Lutyens, the architect of the London Whitehall monument) with three electric trams and a handful of Rochdalians completing the scene.

Memories of Rochdale

Beer is best

A thought-provoking photograph from the 1930s of Lord Street with the Waterworks offices and Salvation Army Citadel on the left, looking across Blackwater Street towards Toad Lane.

Some of the advertisements on the building here make interesting reading: 'Beer is Best' and Rowntrees Cocoa builds bone and muscle' are my favourites - but remember - glasses are no use in the dark, so use not less than 100 watts in a reading lamp when completing your application form for the League of Ovaltineys.

This is one of the earliest photographs of Rochdale Town Hall in existence, taken sometime between 1833 and 1871, showing the original wooden spire and the open river in the foreground. It is notable that the scene is strangely devoid of passers-by.

Rochdale town centre, not-so-long ago...

Left: Memories from the days when smart young Bobbies manned the zebra crossing from The Walk to South Parade. The Burton building on the right of the picture was similar in style to scores of premises owned and operated by the popular tailors throughout the country. This photograph was taken in March 1967 by Clifford C. Ashton who was doing nothing more artistic than trying out his new camera at the time.

Right: This view over the roof-tops was captured in the mid 1960s. The A.B.C cinema dominates the scene - just in front of Hardman's Mill. The open space on the right of the cinema used to be occupied by Kelsall and Kemps Mill until it was demolished in 1962. Also worthy of note are the many bus shelters necessary in the centre before the construction of the central bus station.

Memories of Rochdale

Right: This view of Manchester Road records the 'birth' of the Inner Ring Road - a major development in Rochdale in the 1960s. Brierley's Mill can just be seen on the extreme left and is now the site of Rochdale College. On the right of the picture, the popular Theatre Hotel is just in view.

Left: A charming photograph, thought to date from the late 1950s or early 1960s, dominated by the Town Hall in the distance and featuring the White Angel and John Bright's statue on the Park Slopes.

Memories of Rochdale

Above: The bottom of Blackwater Street and the Duke of Wellington before it was closed in the 1970s.

Above left: The familiar Yorkshire Penny Bank buildings.

Left: St Mary's Gate, the Victorian Chapel, the original Pioneer Co-op offices, Toad Lane and St Mary's Church peeping over the rooftops in the distance

Postcards from the past...

Above: The river Roch before it was covered - seen here around 1900.
Below: A popular view of the old Post Office and John Bright's statue.

Above left: A huge expanse of cobbles along Broadway in this atmospheric view soon after the river was covered over. The covering of the river was a major undertaking at the time as the structure had to withstand enormous loads.
Below: Crowds gather to celebrate the opening of Falinge Park in 1905

Memories of Rochdale

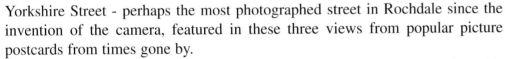

Yorkshire Street - perhaps the most photographed street in Rochdale since the invention of the camera, featured in these three views from popular picture postcards from times gone by.

Many well known retail and commercial businesses have been located on this busy street over the years - and some are still with us. Famous names like *Seniors* the outfitters, *The Yorkshire Penny Bank*, *Yates' Wine Lodge*, the *Bon-Bon*, and *James Duckworth Ltd* greengrocers have had a happy association with this part of Rochdale.

Shopping is an important element in the make-up of any town or city, and changing habits influence the architecture and infrastructure of an area. In the north of England as a whole the 1960s saw dramatic changes occur in the centre of most towns of a similar size to Rochdale. The construction of concrete shopping centres in the heart of town, centralised bus stations, the dominance of the motor car, the rise of the supermarket and demise of corner-shops were all phenomena which crept up on us in the 60s and 70s. These changes were to affect Rochdale a little later than many other towns in the north, but affect her they did. In some towns and cities there is a movement back to the days of *proper shopping* as more and more people look back on them with fondness.

Memories of Rochdale

Postcards from Whitworth

Three very attractive postcards here from the Whitworth area. Incidentally, anyone interested in nostalgia would be well advised to visit the Whitworth Heritage Museum, North Street, Whitworth, which is run on a voluntary basis by members of the Whitworth Historical Society. There are excellent displays of all kinds of household, industrial and other interesting exhibits which put some of the professionally-run establishments to shame. My children loved the visit and everyone is made welcome by the volunteers who proudly show off their museum on Tuesday evenings (7.30pm - 9.30pm) and Saturdays 2.00pm - 4.00pm) 'Phone them first to ensure that stated times are still current, on 01706 853049.

Gone, but not forgotten..

Right: Water Street in the mid 1960s. Most of the buildings seen here have long since gone. On the right of the picture a sign indicates the location of a Jaguar Dealership - it is now the location of a motorcycle dealer. A lot of the site was landscaped and a car park occupies part of the area now.

Below: Wellfield Mill seen in 1966. This area of Oldham Road saw significant changes around this time - one of which being the demolition of the mill itself.. Note the letters 'EWS' on the fence next to the telephone box. They denote "Emergency Water Supply" and were painted in yellow letters next to the tanks of water used for fire-fighting purposes during war time air-raids.

Below right: Yorkshire Street, opposite Cheetham Street. The buildings survived the blight of the 1960s but were knocked down to make way for the Wheatsheaf Shopping Centre.

The photographs on this and the facing page were taken by Allan Marshall in the mid 1960s.

A potted history of the Hornets

The Rochdale Hornets Club was founded in 1871 and gained a well-respected name in Lancashire rugby league circles until the 'breakaway' in 1895 when they became founder members of The Northern Union.

Success on the field was elusive in the early days of the new formation, but after becoming a company in 1906, Hornets slowly, but surely became a force to be reckoned with. Some astute signings, mainly from West Country Rugby Union areas, provided the base for what was to become the club's 'golden era' which culminated in winning the Northern Union Cup in 1921-1922.

On the way to this peak they won the Lancashire Cup in 1911-1912, 1914-1915 and 1918-1919 (also appearing in the finals of 1912-1913 and 1919-1920)

won the Lancashire League in 1918-1919 and figured in the 'top four' play-offs in 1914-1915.

Decline in the 1920s

Thereafter, in the late twenties there was a steady decline, although they did appear in the Rugby League Cup Semi-Final of 1924-25. Then followed a mini-revival in the early and middle thirties led by Mr G. A. Close, a local businessman, but when this petered out another slump left the club fighting for its existence. In the period just before the Second World War the supporters club played a leading role in keeping the club in being. Since the War the Hornets have had an up and down existence, mainly down, but brightened up by short periods of success. They reached the semi-final of the Rugby League Cup in the 1947-1948 and 1957-1958, also reaching the Lancashire Cup Final in 1965-1966

In the seventies the team was coached by two of the most influential ex-players in Frank Myler and Kel Coslett. Under Myler, Hornets reached the final of the B.B.C floodlit competition in 1971-1972 and the final of the John Player Trophy in 1973-74. With the advent of two divisions in 1973-74, Hornets began in the first division but were then relegated three times and promoted twice in the ensuing seasons.

In the early eighties the club's fortunes again deteriorated resulting in the sale of

Courtesy Alpha Photography, Rochdale

the Athletic Grounds and move to Spotland Stadium. This chance brought about a revival and, in 1989-1990 Hornets won promotion to the first division but were sent back quickly due to a disastrous season. Since then they have remained in the forefront of the second division clubs and won a place in the Lancashire Cup Final of 1991-1992. After such a long and chequered history the hope must be that the best is yet to come.

Colin Atkin

Courtesy Alpha Photography, Rochdale

Above: The successful 1922 cup final team.
Above, right: George A. Prudence with the 1919 Lancashire

Rochdale's boxing champion

Jock McAvoy, Rochdale's most accomplished boxer, was, in his day, as famous as Gracie Fields. Nicknamed the *Rochdale Thunderbolt* he used to fight at Belle Vue, Manchester in the 1930s and was a World Title Contender. McAvoy used to run the Brunswick Pub and had a reputation for a bit of a temper. Sadly he succumbed to polio and ended his career signing cards like the one above for fans on the seafront at Blackpool.

Rochdale Pioneers Museum

SEE HOW YOUR ANCESTORS
DID THEIR SHOPPING

Visit the birthplace of the
world-wide Co-operative Movement.
See the original Rochdale Pioneers'
Shop in Toad Lane

Open Tuesday to Saturday **10am - 4pm**
Sundays: **2pm - 4pm.** *Groups welcome by appointment*

Co-operative Union Ltd, Holyoake House, Hanover Street,

Manchester M60 0AS. Tel: 0161 832 4300

Sandbrook Park Rochdale
the home of Co-operative
a national force in retailing

Co-operative Retail Services Ltd
Sandbrook Park
Sandbrook Way
Rochdale
OL11 1SA

co-operative

Cradle of the Co-operative Movement

Rochdale is famous for being the 'home' of the worldwide Co-operative Movement, which started life at No 31 Toad Lane in the humble premises first opened as a shop by the Rochdale Equitable Pioneers Society in December 1844.

The little store established by the Pioneers began by selling only a basic stock of commodities such as butter, sugar, flour, oatmeal and candles, a reflection of the desperate conditions for most working people at the time. Trade developed rapidly however, and within a few years the Pioneers Society was able to open branch shops in other parts of the town - the first was in Oldham Road - and to move into an imposing four storey 'central store' higher up Toad Lane.

Unfortunately this building was demolished to make way for a new road system. But an even more imposing symbol of the Co-operative Movement's success during the intervening years has arrived in Rochdale with the opening in 1996 of a spectacular new headquarters at Sandbrook Park for the largest independent consumer-owned society, CRS Ltd. This has brought hundreds of new jobs to the town and provided a significant boost to the local economy.

The Co-operative Movement that

was born in Rochdale has spread throughout the United Kingdom and today it is one of the country's biggest retail organisations, providing eight million members with a vast range of shopping facilities and services, extending from banking and insurance to travel and funerals. The idea has flourished too as an international network of 750 million members in more than 100 countries, with the 'Rochdale Principles' - the decisions and practices of the first Pioneers - still referred to as a guide to setting up and running co-operative enterprises.

The original Toad Lane premises meanwhile have been lovingly restored as part of a conservation area. Now the Rochdale Pioneers Museum is a source of interest and inspiration for co-operators everywhere attracting thousands of visitors from the UK and abroad each year.

Left: Visitors to the Rochdale Pioneers Museum are struck by the basic simplicity of the original Co-operative store, where the goods initially sold were few. Close inspection of the poster on the wall reveals the Pioneer Principles, which included: open membership, democratic control and political and religous neutrality.

Above: A large crowd gathered at the Pioneers' original store in Toad Lane, to celebrate the co-operative centenary on 21 December 1944

Memories of Rochdale

Centuries of History with a modern approach

How many Rochdalians are there who when passing the group of stalls erected each weekend at the foot of Yorkshire Street remember that they mark the site of Rochdale's first market?

Somewhere about that spot stood the ancient Market Cross (the head of which is now in our Museum), and there, on the appointed days, were to be seen farmer's wives and daughters with baskets of dairy produce. The history of Rochdale markets goes back a long way. Seven hundred years ago in the reign of Henry III, that monarch granted a charter to Edmund de Lascy authorising him to hold a weekly market and an annual fair in Rochdale. For hundreds of years the roadside at the spot mentioned was all that was necessary as a market place.

In 1822, Lord Byron, the poet, sold the old

"Grant to Edmund de Lascy, King's Yeoman and his heirs of a weekly market on Wednesday at this manor of Racchedal, which Margaret, Countess of Lincoln, holds of him in dower; and of a yearly fair there on a vigil, the feast and the morrow of S S Simon & Jude".

market place and the rights he had to it to a local gentleman for £500. A company had come into being, formed by local residents and this was how the Rochdale Market Company was born.

At that time, owing to the ever increasing volume of traffic and the extent to which Yorkshire Street was clogged up on Market days, a need for another site was identified. The company secured the old market place and the land which now forms the site of the lower market and the covered market and in 1824 they erected the present Market Hall at a cost of £30,000.

As the years passed, the hand of change was ceaseless. Some Rochdalians will remember the pig market being held every fortnight and the days when the horse fair was held in Cheetham Street.

The Corporation bought the rights to the Market in 1936 from the old Rochdale Market Company and in 1975 Rochdale's second market hall was demolished to make way for the existing market and the adjoining Shopping Centre which was opened by Prince Phillip, Duke of Edinburgh in that same year.

Below Left: Royal Charter granted to the Lord of the Manor of Rochdale in 1251.
Below: An early picture of the Market stalls on Yorkshire Street.

A modern identity for a 21st Century Shopping Centre

The Rochdale Exchange Shopping Centre was built in two stages. Phase I began in 1975 and Phase II in 1976. It was officially opened by Gracie Fields on 15th September 1978.

The cost of the building was in the region of £6 million. Today, 250,000 customers walk through its doors and the car park's 850 space facility caters for 10,000 vehicles each week.

Rochdale Exchange Shopping Centre, Rochdale's premier shopping centre offers a wide variety of stores with many major national retailers, a Market Hall and a covered Market.

The shopping centre was originally known as Rochdale Shopping Centre but this was changed to its present name in July 1995 when refurbishment work on the building began and saw the basically drab building enhanced to a brighter facade and a more modern interior. A name and logo for the

centre were required to reflect this new image

Exchange suggests the trading of goods, which is as significant to the people of Rochdale today as it was to the Journeyman Weavers or Co-operative Pioneers of the past.

Refurbishment has provided the opportunity to change the image and quality of the centre - for a modern identity which will take it into the 21st century.

Above: The new-look Rochdale Exchange Shopping Centre. Work on renovating the drab building carried on throughout 1995 and 1996 and finished in early 1997. The work entailed removing the old fashioned, unsightly tiles and replacing it with attractive modern brickwork.

Left: Michael Howard, Home Secretary, visiting Rochdale Exchange Shopping Cenre recently. Also pictured here is Mike Matthews, the Centre Manager, who is showing Mr Howard the security system.

TEXTILES

Technical textile solutions for today's arduous environments

TBA Industrial Products Ltd
TBA Textiles, P.O. Box 40
Rochdale OL12 7EQ
Tel: 01706 47422
Fax: 01706 712283

TBA Industrial Products Ltd is part of T & N PLC

TBA Textiles has more than 125 years experience in the development, manufacture and supply of specialist products to combat and protect from today's arduous environments. TBA's wealth of knowledge, underpinned by sound marketing expertise, enables today's customers to select from a range of products capable of satisfying very diverse and specialised requirements.

Fire protection textiles contribute substantially to TBA's business, including applications such as fire barriers to stop the spread of smoke and flame, keeping safe visitors to historical buildings such as Colchester Castle, and retail sites such as Marks and Spencers. Fire fighters from Australia and New Zealand use TBA Textiles' fabric to line uniforms to safeguard them from heat and flames, and anti-vandal, fire-resistant seating protects commuters every day on the London Underground and the German State Railway.

Ballistic advancements have led to hard armour protection for bomb disposal units for the Ministry of Defence. The development of stab and bullet-proof jackets used not only by police forces and the ambulance service, but also by troops serving with UN peace-keeping forces ensures the safety of those employed to protect others.

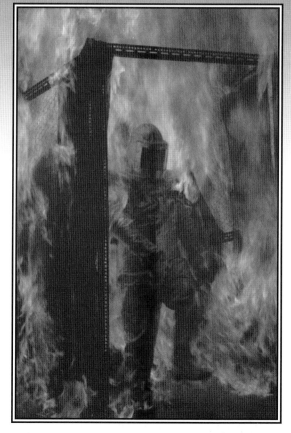

TBA Textiles

The Turner family started manufacturing cotton cloth in the Spotland district in 1885, but it was in 1871 that three sons of Samuel Turner formed the company of Turner Brothers to manufacture packings from cotton cloth for steam pipes.

It was not until 1878 that asbestos in large quantities was discovered following a disastrous forest fire. The first consignment reached Rochdale the following year and the Turner Brothers marketed the first machine-processed asbestos goods within a year after that.

During the next 40 years, the company enjoyed its success and adopted Limited liability status in 1899, changing its name to Turner Brothers Asbestos Co. Ltd in 1916. TBA steadily expanded until 1920, when the company amalgamated with three other leading

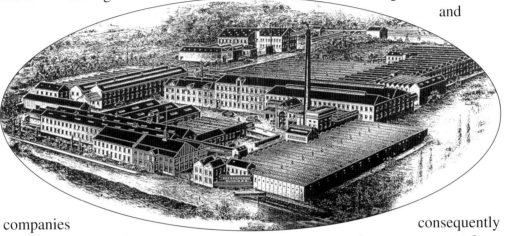

companies in the industry to form Turner Newall Ltd. This group has grown quickly and now ranks as one of the largest industrial companies in Great Britain, owning many companies world-wide. During and immediately after the First World War, the company's products were in great demand and consequently the company went from strength to strength. The business prospered to such an extent that in its heyday the factory occupied a 60 acre site and employed over 3000 people. With the collapse of the market for its traditional products, TBA turned its attention to emerging new fields demanding skill and enterprise such as the spinning and weaving of glass. TBA Industrial Products was spilt into three autonomous businesses, which have since grown to a total of five market-focused, independent and profitable companies under the names of TBA Textiles, TBA Composites, Flexitallic Sealing Materials, Bentley Harris and TBA Electro-Conductive Products. All sharing the original site, the continual developments and investment in training have released a surge of energy and creativity as new opportunities have been opened up and explored to meet today's ever expanding customer needs.

RATCLIFFES OF ROCHDALE

75 years of service

1922 - 1997

Ratcliffes of Rochdale have been serving their customers for 75 years, ever since the Ratcliffe Brothers opened the Mount Garage on Halifax Road in 1922.

The garage is still in the hands of the same family and still offers the same care, service, quality and value for money for which Ratcliffes have become recognised over the past 75 years.

If your car needs **servicing**, **repairing** or **painting**, come to Ratcliffes of Rochdale, because

Ratcliffes Care - about your car!

If you are looking for a new or used car, come to Ratcliffes of Rochdale, because

Ratcliffes Care - about you!

Ratcliffes Care

Ratcliffes of Rochdale · Mount Garage · Halifax Road · Rochdale
Tel: 01706 373021

75 years of Motoring History

In 1997 Ratcliffes of Rochdale celebrates 75 years of service. The company was founded in 1922, on the same site as the present garage - though now much changed and enlarged - at Mount Green Garage, Halifax Road, Rochdale, opposite Birch Hill Hospital.

Ratcliffes is a family owned business and as such is the oldest in Rochdale, in the hands of the same family. Over the years Ratcliffes have had an exciting and challenging history. One of the founder brothers Bert, was a renowned speedway rider and enjoyed much success on local tracks while brother Harold was once famous for stopping horses! As a young man, he was travelling in a van with one of his brothers when a wheel came off, startling a greengrocers horse and causing it to bolt - complete with cart and load. The brothers gave chase and Harold managed to jump on board the swaying cart and bring it to a halt. The greengrocer was so grateful for his efforts, he rewarded Harold with an apple!

In its early years the company serviced and repaired motor cycles and cars, as well as selling petrol, in the days when petrol was sold in cans. In fact, the garage was one of the first in the area to have petrol pumps installed. The petrol station side was extended and updated over the next few years and was eventually sold so that Ratcliffes could concentrate on car sales, servicing and repairs.

Above: A line up of Morris cars outside Ratcliffe's Workshops. *Below:* This Mini was entered in a float in the late 1960s. *Below left:* The original petrol pumps. Ratcliffes were one of the first to install them.

Citroen Main Dealer

Now a Citroen main dealer, Ratcliffe Brothers, as it was originally known, started off with a Morris agency in 1934 and over the years has sold Wolsley, MG and Vanden Plas cars plus many more.

In 1978 they became Opel dealers, including the Vauxhall range when the two companies joined in 1980.

P W Greenhalgh & Co Ltd
Over 90 years of Textile Treatment

The original buildings on the Ogden Mill site were acquired around 1903 by Andrew Greenhalgh, a well known mill owner and philanthropist at that time. He bought the site for two of his sons, Phillip William and Arthur. The original mill was a woollen fulling works but under the new ownership it was converted to a cotton piece goods dyeing and finishing works. The site was ideally placed, having a good and plentiful supply of water from the Corporation reservoirs up the valley from the mill and an excellent supply of coal.

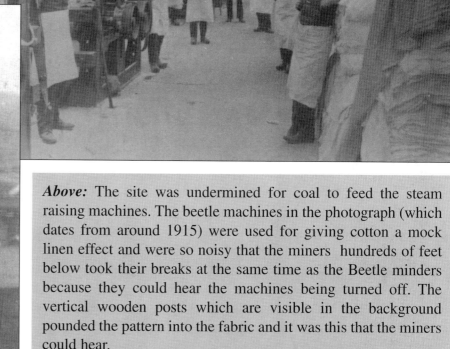

Above: The site was undermined for coal to feed the steam raising machines. The beetle machines in the photograph (which dates from around 1915) were used for giving cotton a mock linen effect and were so noisy that the miners hundreds of feet below took their breaks at the same time as the Beetle minders because they could hear the machines being turned off. The vertical wooden posts which are visible in the background pounded the pattern into the fabric and it was this that the miners could hear.

Left: The Ogden Mill site, taken around 1913. The mine workings can be seen in the foreground to the left of the photograph.

Memories of Rochdale

develop polymer coatings for garment interlinings, and were the first to develop acrylic coatings for thermal and blackout curtains for the hotel trade in the U.K. The present day advantage of the site is its ease of access to the M62 and Manchester.

Left: Another view of the Ogden Mill site.
Below: This picure dates from 1920 and in those days workers, which as the picture shows, included boys, were sent home for being a minute late and P W Greenhalgh himself, who lived opposite, was reputed by the employees to be able to recognise late arriving workers by the sound of their wooden clogs on the cobbles in the yard.

In the early years of the business, the company ran its own mining operation to feed coal to the steam raising plant. Of course, steam was not only required to provide the heating for the bleaching chemicals but also to run the steam engine which provided the mechanical power for the machinery.

During the Second World War, Greenhalgh's made plaster cloths for the military, as well as carrying on their usual trade in doing so. The mining of their own coal stopped at this time also, as the coal was needed elsewhere. The mill prospered during the war when it was producing heavily for the armed services.

In the 1960s, Greenhalgh's moved into the more technical side of fabric treatment and were one of the first companies in Britain to

Memories of Rochdale

Until the late 1920s a horse-drawn wagon used to travel to Manchester to deliver the finished goods and to collect loomstate for processing. He would have a tot for breakfast in the nearby Bull's Head public house before his journey to Manchester, which began at 5.30 every morning. Nowadays, the mill produces over 500,000 metres every week and, on average, fifteen to twenty wagons are loaded and unloaded there every day.

The first products were shirtings for Africa, and after the Second World War, Silesias, pocketing fabrics, canvas and similar fabrics.

The mill has developed from being a simple bleaching and dyeing factory to a high tech bleachers, dyers, finishers and coating operation employing 160 people.

Since the current directors took over in the seventies the product line has moved towards ever more technical finishing. This started with the production of easy care finishes for shirt interlinings and then the coating of polythene adhesives onto the interlining fabrics.

Since then it has moved on further through several other developments to the foam coating of curtain and upholstery fabric with flame retardant and blackout acrylic foam finishes. However, traditional sateen curtains are still an important aspect to the company's production lines.

The company is now in its fourth generation of family ownership. In the 40s Andrew Phillip William Greenhalgh took over from his father and then almost twenty years later, his sons Michael and Peter joined the business, taking over from their father. In 1986 their sons Simon and Ben joined the Company.

Above: An open lorry decorated for a carnival in Morecambe in the less politically correct 1960s. It won First Prize in the event.

Left: This photograph dates from the turn of the century and shows three men standing on the steps of a steam wagon.

From clogs to architectural woodwork and timber in 160 years

Fletcher Bolton Ltd., Timber Merchants was founded in 1830 by the original Fletcher Bolton. The firm's principal business is timber merchanting and bespoke machining. However it began life as a Clog Makers and from these humble beginnings of cutting down alder trees to make clog soles, huge sawmills are now owned by the company on a three acre site in Oldham Road, Rochdale. It wasn't long before the desire for clogs began dying out and the timber merchanting side started to take over. Records show that in 1915 there were about 35 employees but soon afterwards these numbers fell to below ten and there was talk of the firm closing. Fortunately this did not happen. Efforts to rebuild and expand were successful and by the end of 1918 it was back to its former glory, employing once again about 35 workers. In 1927, the company became a private limited company with Mr Fletcher Bolton,

the founder's grandson, at the helm as governing director. At this time a horse and cart did the heavy work. Today sideloaders do the yard work and heavy goods vehicles are used for deliveries. 1977 saw the move to new premises on Wood street and in 1986 Timbmet Ltd (the country's largest independent hardwood importer) took over. Adding to an already large product range, they introduced hardwoods and veneered sheet materials. Further expansion saw the building of a new Trade and Retail collection centre. These days the workforce totals 134 and their customer base has expanded from the Rochdale area to cover the whole of the country. Further plans will set the foundations for future growth and Fletcher Bolton continuing into the year 2000.

Above: the company's employees line up for a photograph in 1952.

Below Left: Fletcher Bolton in the foreground with Rochdale stretching out behind.

DEVELOPING THE PIONEER SPIRIT

Taylor Patterns in Walker Sreet in 1955, with Roy Taylor's Austin Sheerline, one of only two cars in the street.

*Managing Director
Rod Taylor*

Scott Taylor and grandfather Roy with Gracie Fields at the present site's opening in October 1970

With 250 employees, Taylor Engineering & Plastics today is a far cry from the two-man business of 1949 and the 80-man business of 1977. In fact, turnover is now over 15 times what it was in the 1970s.

The business has grown because the Taylors have always believed in high levels of investment, offering clients the state-of-the-art in moulding technology. Plant has been added continuously to meet new demands.

A second site was bought in 1979 at Queensway to help expand production, since when TEP has developed a full 'design to delivery' service built on computer aided design and manufacture.

Not only does this overcome the need for client drawings of the product to be moulded, but it means TEP can take the process right through to finishing and assembly with other products.

Still using its traditional experience as toolmakers, including prototype tooling, TEP has separate operating divisions for each major area of production: Polyurethanes, Thermoplastic Structural Foam and Thermoplastic Injection Moulding.

Now the UK leader in its field, TEP has every right to its title of the 'Polymer Moulding Pioneers'.

TEP
T A Y L O R
Engineering & Plastics
Ltd

Taylor Engineering & Plastics Limited
Molesworth Street • Rochdale • Lancashire • OL16 2BD • ENGLAND
Telephone: 01706 714700 • Facsimile: 01706 714707

Taylor's: off the ground with just £100!

In 1949 money went an awful lot further than it does now. Nearly 50 years before the Taylor Engineering & Plastics of today, a gift of £100 to Roy Taylor from his mother Lucy was enough for him to set up in business, and Taylor's Patterns was born in the old Wesleyan chapel in Holland Street.

With Roy bringing in the work from the foundry industry and helping his first employee, Charlie Hopwood to turn out the patterns, by the early 1950s there were enough orders to move to new premises in Walker Street. Now also making lasts for the shoe and slipper industry in the 'valley' around Bacup and Burnley, numbers started to grow.

Boom time came from making patterns and supplying the moulds for latex foam cushions for upholstery and cars for the likes of Vitafoam and Dunlop. By 1959, when Roy's son Rod started in the Walker Street mill at 15, there were already 30 pattern makers there - a large number by any standards.

When Vitafoam's Don Mill in Middleton burned down at the start of the 60s, Taylor's had to work hard to replace the lost moulds, and in 1964 the company became Vitool, a British Vita subsidiary.

The Walker Street Mill was knocked down to become the car park for new works and offices opened on 27th October 1970 by Gracie Fields.

Gracie did the honours because Roy Taylor knocked on the door of her house in Capri during a Mediterranean cruise, and backed by the British Vita Silver Band, she sang 'Sally' outside on the grass at Molesworth Street.

In 1977 father and son bought the business back and Roy retired in favour of Rod, who is still managing director of the TEP of today. The family tradition continues as strong as ever, with his wife Jean also a director and their son Scott joining in 1994.

Below & right: Making the mould for latex foam cushions in the 50s

Above: Vicar's Moss Works, Walker Street in the 1950s

Memories of Rochdale

Rochdale-made transmission equipment for the world market

W R Anderton was founded by three brothers and began trading before the Second World War. The company manufactures clutches and power take-off equipment for well known diesel engine manufacturers like Perkins, Dorman Diesels and Lister Diesels. During the War Stanley Etherington, was awarded the M.B.E. for Service to Industry. He was to acquire a majority shareholding in the company in 1955. The following year Stanley's son, Roy joined the firm due to his father's failing health.

The company continued to manufacture clutches and take-off equipment until 1975 when Roy Etherington set up W R Anderton Precision Gears on Regent Street in Rochdale. At that time the company employed more than 140 people and was a national leader in its field.

Three years later the company

W.R. Anderton's famed power take-off units awaiting dispatch.

took advantage of favourable trading conditions and set up N C Laser Cutting Service at Cark in Cumbria using state of the art technology for sub contract laser cutting. After serving his apprenticeship at Regent Street, Roy's son Stuart went on to manage the Cumbria plant where he is still based today.

In 1983 Accu-Rout was set up, to be run by the present joint MD Mark Etherington, at Hamer, Rochdale. It remained at Hamer until the death of Roy Etherington in 1987. At this time Accu-Rout was moved to Castleton and the Regent Street business was sold.

The company is now considered to be the largest sub-contract laser shop in the UK.

A programme of investment in plant and equipment has meant that the focus of the business has moved away from transmission equipment towards the development of more general sub-contract engineering. However, transmission equipment is still produced in smaller numbers and the company is always investigating new product lines and services.

The canal-side location of W.R. Anderton circa 1970

Memories of Rochdale

Lovick's was founded in 1919 by William Lovick. Originally the company traded as Lovick and Beaumont and was funded by money given as a gratuity when William was demobbed from the army after World War I.

Based in Yorkshire Street in what was originally the Station Hotel and then later the T.B. Clinic, Lovick's has traded from the same street since its foundation.

Over the years Lovick's has prospered because of its ability to see opportunities and seize them. One example is that during the 30s, when the Ceylon Picture House on the same Street was showing its films, the Cinema goers would have to walk past Lovick's on their way home. The company soon recognised the potential and began staying open until 11 pm to catch them!

The first van they acquired was a Model T pick-up which was used to travel to Hebden Bridge to collect stock, back in the days when automobiles were a novelty. At first there were problems though - the engine boiled up on every single journey and nobody could understand why. It was later explained that the van had gears!

Now Lovicks is owned by a third generation of the family, Bill, whose son, David and daughter, Helen are also in the business. A fifth generation has just been born. As always their aim has been to give the customer satisfaction and the security that four generations of the company have collected and pooled their knowledge and expertise to give the customer exactly what they want.

Memories of Rochdale

Hanson Springs started manufacturing springs for the textile industry in 1963. The company was founded by Malcolm Hanson who was just 18 years old. The first factory was based at Marland Forge, Rochdale.

Four years later the company outgrew its premises and moved to larger ones at Heywood where they became an incorporated company, Expanding all the time, Hanson Springs Limited moved twice again within the next ten years finally ending up at Lincoln Street (below). Mellor Street in Rochdale (right) was purchased in 1995.

In 1979 Hanson Springs began exporting its products to Europe, quickly followed by North America, Australia, Asia and Africa. Nowadays, the percentage of the total produce which is exported stands at 55%.

During its thirty four year history the company has seen many changes but the ideas of the directors have not changed, this being the pursuit of manufacturing the highest quality product at all times. Over the years this policy has led to a great deal of pride within the company which is evident in the finished product.

Now Hanson Springs does not only supply to

the textile industry but to a wide range of industries including Oil, Energy, Chemical and Prime Movers.

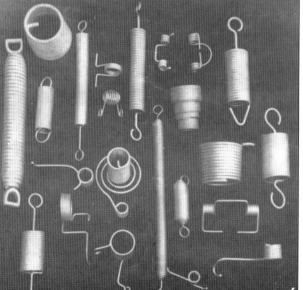

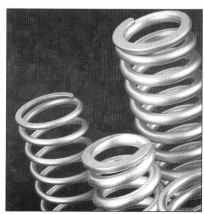

Live-wires celebrate 50 years in Rochdale

Auto Battery Service (ABS) was founded in 1946 by Fred Warham and Tom Smith. Moses Smith, father of Tom worked for Oldham Batteries in Denton and let Fred and Tom know that Oldham were looking to set up a network of battery service centres. This was in the days when old batteries were rebuilt and not just thrown away. This valuable piece of 'inside' information led to the formation of ABS and over 50 successful years supplying the motor trade. As time went on, the company diversified into all kinds of automotive parts and nowadays some of Europe's leading brand names are supplied by ABS to the motor trade.

John Warham, son of Fred Warham recounts the story of the days when battery connectors were soldered to vehicles on the street outside the original premises in St Mary's Gate (see photo below). The soldering iron was heated in the fire which was in the back room upstairs, carried down the stairs, through the shop and out to the waiting vehicle, at which point it was often too cool to use! Thankfully, technology has moved on. Today, ABS prides itself on supplying the cream of auto-component brands and looks forward with enthusiasm to the prospect of serving the motoring needs of Rochdale for at least another 50 years.

HENLYS FORD
of Rochdale

Rochdale Motor Garage Limited was formed in 1922 by local business men and after going from strength to strength for almost a decade, it acquired the Ford franchise in 1931, becoming the main Ford dealer.

Meanwhile, in 1928 Henlys was being founded by Bertie Henly. He was considered to be one of the greatest entrepreneurs of his time and was deeply involved with the design and finance of the first Jaguar car.

In 1953, Tom Mellor, who had his own motor dealership and car hire business called Tom Mellor Limited, acquired shares in Rochdale Motor Garage Limited and developed the business.

Tom Mellor was a prominent citizen in Manchester at the time and was Mayor of Salford, although he actually lived on the outskirts of Rochdale at Sautridge House.

In 1959, the company realised that it needed to expand and acquired the building belonging to H Rothwell Limited which

ideally, was next door. This building was later converted into the parts department. Premises were also bought on Oldham Road adjacent to LC Hilliers and these were converted into a car body building business.

In 1980 Mr Hillier decided to sell his dealership and Rochdale Motor Garage, trading as Tom Mellor

Ford realised that this was an opportunity they could not afford to miss. They bought Mr Hillier out and moved their premises onto the busy Oldham Road.

After the death of Tom Mellor, his family decided to move to the Channel Isles and Henlys quickly put in an offer for the business. It was accepted and the company now successfully trades as Henlys Ford of Rochdale - part of Henlys PLC

75 years of Quality Motoring

HENLYS FORD
of Rochdale

New & Used Vehicles

Ford Fleet Sales

Transit Specialist Dealer

Car and Van Servicing

MOT Testing (Class 4 & 7)

Ford Accident Repair Specialist

Large Parts Department

Ford Rent-A-Car (And Van)

Local Business Specialist

Henlys Ford of Rochdale,

Oldham Road, Rochdale,
Lancashire OL11 1BU
Tel: 01706 355355
Fax: 01706 527709

Nearly 80 years of Quality Clothing in Rochdale

Est. 1919
Seniors
ABSOLUTELY UNEQUALLED
'Has stood the test for years'

A family business which began in Rochdale almost 80 years ago providing suits for the town's young men returning from the First World War, is still serving their families today.

In fact, Seniors of Rochdale have provided a style for the fashion conscious people of Rochdale, which is unrivalled in its 77 year history.

Today, owner Tony Senior can look back with pride on a history of service to the community which has encouraged up to four generations of the same local families to come back and shop at Seniors year after year.

The Early Years

Mr Senior recalls: " My father, Sydney Senior arrived in Rochdale in 1919 and rented rooms above the men's outfitters of S Exley Wild at the corner of number 28, Yorkshire Street and number 1, Baillie Street.

"He began in business by making made-to-measure suits for the men coming home at the end of the 1914-18 war.

The Three Guinea Suit

"In those days it cost them just three guineas for a top quality suit which was made in just two weeks in our workroom - faster than anywhere else in the town.

"And after khaki, it seemed that all the soldiers wanted was a blue serge suit!"

In 1921 Sydney Senior bought the shop below his rented rooms from Exley Wild and in an unprecedented expansion due to the success of business he purchased several other shops to provide the large store that Seniors has become today.

Senior Service

From those early days the owner's motto has been to give the people of Rochdale 'Senior Service', in other words the very best in both goods and personal service to its customers.

And that still applies today, thanks to the leadership of Tony Senior, who joined the family business in 1958.

Since he took over, the business has seen a major expansion into menswear and the introduction of a superb ladies wear department. But seventy seven years on the family motto remains the same: "We always aim to give Senior Service."

No matter how fashion and trends change over the years designers names come and go, Seniors quality always stays reliable.

Below: Senior's shop is centre stage in this scene of celebration

Memories of Rochdale

Bathroom pioneers for almost 70 years

Seeley's Bathrooms was started in 1927 by two brothers, John and Henry Seeley. One a plasterer and the other a plumber working in the Rochdale area.

The first premises they owned were beside St Mary's Church, a listed building. At this time they specialised in removing the old black-leaded stoves and replaced them with modern tiled fireplaces.

Before long, people were throwing their old tin baths away and for the first time had baths fitted with hot and cold running water. Along with these came inside toilets.

Pure Luxury

This was considered to be pure luxury because it meant no more trips down the yard in the depths of winter, in the middle of night armed only with a torch or lamp. At the time only the priviledged few owned such luxury but nowadays it is rare to find a house without an inside loo.

These days Bathrooms have progressed onto Jacuzzi baths and steam and power showers. I wonder what people from the turn of the century would make of those!

With experience that spans from the twenties you can guarantee that Seeley's are there with just the right advice for your needs.

Seeley's now own an extensive showroom on the same site as the original showroom with over twenty five bathroom suites on display ranging from the extravagant to the more basic budget ranges. There are also Jacuzzis, Teuco Baths and steam and power showers on display in the bright, modern premises.

Isherwoods: one of Rochdale's longest established companies.

Founded in 1861 by James Henry Isherwood as oil blenders and lubricant producers, the company traded originally as J H Isherwood & Company from premises at Heybrook Corner, but by 1885 they had moved to their present premises on Entwisle Road. The cotton and engineering industries were in rapid expansion in the late 19th century and Isherwoods primarily produced lubricants for all types of machinery. In 1928 a Limited Company was formed and at that time Isherwood's described themselves as 'Oil, Grease & Paint Merchants'. In the early 1900s, most paints were mixed by hand from powders or colours in oil and were often prepared from a white lead paste base.

An order form dating from the 1930s shows the Company's range of products at the time, ranging from Double Boiled Linseed Oil to Beam and Bobbin Enamel.

Ready mixed shades of branded decorative paints although manufactured for some years were not widely available until the late 40s when ICI "Dulux" and other famous names came into prominence.

Isherwood's became stockists of these products and by the early 60s oil manufacture had ceased.

Today, Isherwood's provide a daily delivery service throughout Greater Manchester and supply a wide range of decorative paints, wallpapers, fabrics and sundries to a broad spectrum of industry of which the professional decorator and painting contractor form a large part.

Over recent years, the company has developed wallpapers and fabric showrooms at both their Rochdale and Oldham branches to offer the benefits of unrivalled choice and competitive prices to the general public. Most leading brands of wallpaper pattern books are on display, together with co-ordinating fabrics. Expect lots of help and friendly advice, the staff are on hand to guide customers in achieving a perfect home.

Above and Left: These dramatic pictures depict the Roch Valley Viaduct being demolished in the 60s. When the arches were felled, one fell across Entwisle Road, which was still open to traffic. People ran for their lives but amazingly nobody was hurt. 2,000 people were evacuated from their homes until the debris could be dealt with some days later.